Great Artists

Claude Monet

ABDO
Publishing Company

Adam G. Klein

Cover Photo: Corbis
Interior Photos: Art Resource pp. 1, 9, 17, 23, 27; Bridgeman Art Library pp. 10, 11, 13, 15, 19,
    25; Corbis p. 29; Getty Images pp. 5, 21

Series Coordinator: Megan M. Gunderson
Editors: Heidi M. Dahmes, Megan M. Gunderson
Cover Design: Neil Klinepier
Interior Design: Dave Bullen

Library of Congress Cataloging-in-Publication Data

Klein, Adam G., 1976-
  Claude Monet / Adam G. Klein.
    p. cm. -- (Great artists)
  Includes index.
  ISBN-10 1-59679-732-0
  ISBN-13 978-1-59679-732-1
  1. Monet, Claude, 1840-1926--Juvenile literature. 2. Painters--France--Biography--Juvenile
literature. 3. Impressionism (Art)--France--Juvenile literature. I. Monet, Claude, 1840-1926. II.
Title III. Series: Klein, Adam G., 1976- . Great artists.

  ND553.M7.K54 2006
  759.4--dc22

                                                                          2005017890

Contents

Claude Monet

In the late 1800s, the world was experiencing many changes. Towns were growing into cities, and life was becoming more modern.

Some artists felt the need to change with the times. Claude Monet was one such artist. He practiced **plein air** painting and transformed the landscape **genre**. Monet had a vision, which led to the start of a new art movement called Impressionism.

Impressionist artists tried to show how objects naturally appear. To do this, they painted using strokes or dabs of primary colors. They also paid close attention to how light reflected off of the objects. In this way, Impressionists hoped to capture moments in time in their paintings.

People did not immediately accept Impressionism. But no matter what **critics** said, Monet kept painting the way he wanted to. As a result, Monet often struggled to sell his work. This is

because it pushed the limits of what society would accept in art. Eventually, people warmed up to his style. And today, exhibits of his work draw crowds of admirers.

Monet was an artist for more than 70 years.

1840 ~ On November 14, Oscar-Claude Monet was born in Paris, France.

1858 ~ Monet exhibited *View of Rouelles* in Le Havre, France.

1865 ~ *The Mouth of the Seine at Honfleur* and *The Pointe de la Hève at Low Tide* were accepted at the Salon.

1866 ~ *Camille (The Green Dress)* and *Road to Chailly* were shown at the Salon.

1867 ~ The Salon jury rejected *Women in the Garden*.

1868 ~ Monet exhibited *Boats Setting Out from the Port of Le Havre* at the Salon.

1869 ~ Monet painted *La Grenouillère*, which is considered one of the first Impressionist works.

1871 ~ In London, Monet painted *Meditation, Madame Monet on the Sofa*.

1880 ~ Monet submitted *The Seine at Lavacourt* and *Floating Ice* to the Salon. *The Seine at Lavacourt* was accepted.

1886 ~ Monet painted *Storm off the Belle-Isle Coast*.

1891 ~ Monet exhibited his grain stacks series.

1922 ~ The French government accepted Monet's water lilies series.

1926 ~ On December 5, Monet died in Giverny.

Fun Facts

- Claude Monet signed his early artwork with the name "Oscar." This was the name his parents called him. However, he began using the name "Claude" to sign his artwork after 1862.

- While Monet was painting a series of poplar trees in 1891, the trees were sold for lumber. Monet paid to have the trees remain uncut until he finished his series.

- In 1907, dust kicked up by passing cars was settling on Monet's water garden. So, he helped pay to have two roads in Giverny paved!

- When Monet's eyesight started to fail, he had trouble distinguishing different colors. So, he chose colors by reading the labels on the paint tubes.

- Throughout his career, Monet often became frustrated with his work. Scholars estimate that he destroyed more than 500 of his own paintings. He did this by slashing the works or by burning them.

By the Ocean

Oscar-Claude Monet was born on November 14, 1840, in Paris, France. He was the second child of Louise-Justine Aubry and Claude Adolphe Monet. In 1845, the Monet family settled near the ocean in Ingouville, France.

In 1851, Claude began attending school. He studied many subjects, including art. Claude soon began creating **caricatures**, which were displayed in the window of a local frame-maker's shop. People quickly recognized their fellow villagers in Claude's drawings! By age 15, he had gained local fame.

Claude continued to pursue his art. He met artist Eugène-Louis Boudin, who introduced him to **plein air** painting. Boudin and Claude spent many hours painting directly from nature. The ocean inspired Claude. He liked the way light reflected off of the scenery. Claude knew he had found his calling in life.

When his caricatures were on display, Monet sometimes stood nearby listening to viewers praise his work.

Determination

Claude's mother died on January 28, 1857. Soon after, the Monet family moved to nearby Le Havre, France. There, Monet displayed his work in 1858. *View of Rouelles* was the first oil painting Monet exhibited.

Monet was soon determined to go to Paris. There, he began studying at the Académie Suisse in February 1860. Many famous artists had worked at the studio. Monet met Camille Pissarro while studying there.

The following year, Monet was **drafted** and sent to Algeria. After a short time, he became sick and had to return home. But the light and colors of northern Africa had inspired Monet. Back in Le Havre, he applied these new colors in the seascapes he painted. Monet later said his experiences in Algeria helped him become an Impressionist.

Artist Charles Lhuillier painted this portrait of Monet in his army uniform.

Monet painted View of Rouelles *during a trip with Boudin. After he met Boudin, Monet never stopped painting outdoors.*

In 1862, Monet began studying with Charles Gleyre. At Gleyre's studio, Monet became friends with Frédéric Bazille, Alfred Sisley, and Pierre-Auguste Renoir. When Gleyre's studio closed in 1864, the students left to paint in the forest of Fontainebleau.

The Salon

Each year, a Paris institution called the Salon held an exhibition. This was an important place for artists to show their work. A panel of judges decided if paintings were good enough to be exhibited. If an artist was chosen for the show, it could advance his or her career.

In 1865, the Salon accepted Monet's work for the first time. The chosen works were *The Mouth of the Seine at Honfleur* and *The Pointe de la Hève at Low Tide*. The following year, Monet enjoyed success with *Camille (The Green Dress)* and *Road to Chailly*.

At both exhibitions, people confused Monet with Édouard Manet. Manet was a more famous artist at the time. The additional publicity helped Monet's career. The two artists met after the 1866 Salon and worked together later in the 1860s.

The Salon had been a good place for Monet's work to be seen. But, it had many rules that Monet did not always follow. His

new work titled *Women in the Garden* was not seen favorably. Monet and many others were rejected from the Salon in 1867. So, Monet left Paris and went to live with his father in Sainte-Adresse, near Le Havre.

Monet's future wife Camille modeled as all the figures for Women in the Garden.

Experimenting

In Sainte-Adresse, Monet worked on paintings for the next Salon. He exhibited *Boats Setting Out from the Port of Le Havre* in 1868. But in 1869, the Salon rejected his work again. During this time, Monet struggled to earn money. Despite his problems, Monet refused to compromise his style.

In 1869, Monet and Renoir worked near the Seine River. They experimented with short brushstrokes and focused on how light reflects on water. *La Grenouillère* is considered one of Monet's first paintings in this new style.

On June 28, 1870, Monet married Camille Doncieux. They had a son named Jean-Armand-Claude. This was a happier time for Monet. However, the threat of war loomed over France. Prussia wanted to rule Spain, and France opposed this. Monet's family moved to Trouville, France, on the English Channel. Monet wanted to live by the coast so they could escape if the conflict heightened into war.

Much like photographs, Monet's paintings often capture moments in time. This can be seen in **The Beach at Trouville.**

In Trouville, Monet continued experimenting with color, brushstrokes, and trying to capture moments in time. While working outdoors, sand from the beach mixed in with his paints. This can still be seen today in *The Beach at Trouville*.

On July 19, the **Franco-Prussian War** began. Soon, many people fled across the English Channel to London, England. Monet's family joined the move.

Rebuilding

In London, Monet painted the Thames River and the Houses of Parliament. He also painted a portrait of Camille. The London fog made it difficult to work outdoors. So in 1871, he painted *Meditation, Madame Monet on the Sofa* indoors.

Monet also made an important connection during his stay. Fellow artist Charles-François Daubigny introduced Monet to art dealer Paul Durand-Ruel. Durand-Ruel was interested in unusual artwork. In May 1871, he purchased Monet's work for the first time.

The **Franco-Prussian War** left Paris in ruins. So the French began to rebuild. After the long years of war, the French looked forward to the future. Many were looking for something new, different, and modern in the reconstruction.

Monet was also looking for something new. So, the family decided to travel to the Netherlands. There, Monet spent a few

Meditation, Madame Monet on the Sofa *is unusual, because Monet typically painted Camille outdoors.*

months painting windmills and canals. The Monets returned to France in autumn 1871. Since Paris was still being rebuilt, they settled in nearby Argenteuil. Monet quickly began painting views of the countryside and his large garden.

Starving Artists

In France, Monet also reunited with Renoir, Pissarro, and Boudin. On April 15, 1874, they joined 26 other artists in an independent exhibition. Their work created a lot of discussion, and the show was successful. Monet exhibited a painting titled *Impression: Sunrise*. Because of this work, the artists were soon being called Impressionists.

Through the years, Monet continued exhibiting with the Impressionists. Unfortunately, he still was not making much money from his art. But in 1876, a wealthy businessman named Ernest Hoschedé **commissioned** four works.

The Monets and the Hoschedés became very close. After financial trouble, Hoschedé left his family. Hoschedé's wife, Alice, and six children moved into Monet's new home in Vétheuil, France. Monet now had two families to support.

In 1877, Camille became ill. She gave birth to their second son, Michel, in 1878. However, she died the following year.

Monet was heartbroken. But, he needed to continue working to provide for the combined household.

Monet had heard that Renoir's career had improved again after submitting paintings to the Salon. Desperate for money, Monet decided to give it a try.

Impression: Sunrise *is a view of Le Havre.*

Success

Submitting work to the Salon meant Monet could not exhibit with the Impressionists. It wasn't a difficult decision for him. He still considered himself an Impressionist. But, he had to do what he could to improve his financial situation.

Monet submitted *The Seine at Lavacourt* and *Floating Ice* to the 1880 Salon jury. The jury accepted *The Seine at Lavacourt*. At the same time, Monet was asked to do a one-man show. After these showings, Monet was finally selling more of his work.

Because of his financial success, Monet could afford a new home in Giverny, France. He also had time to travel. So in December 1883, he went to the Mediterranean Sea with Renoir to sightsee and paint. The southern sun inspired Monet in new ways. He created bright and colorful paintings of the region.

*Today, visitors to Giverny can see Monet's house
and gardens as they appeared during his lifetime.*

Monet's success continued. He began painting different versions of the same scene. Monet worked on several paintings in a day. He changed the painting he was working on depending on where the sun was in the sky. This plan allowed him to finish more paintings.

New Themes

In 1886, Durand-Ruel sent some of Monet's paintings to New York City, New York. Monet was not sure this was a good idea. So, he was surprised when people in America were excited about his paintings. Monet's work sold well, and he was now known internationally.

The struggles Monet had experienced early in his career were long gone. His work was widely accepted, and a new generation of **rebels** was replacing him. Many of these new artists had looked to the Impressionists for inspiration.

Like these new artists, Monet continued to challenge society's perception of art. There were still new themes for him to paint. In 1886, Monet traveled to paint storms on the northwestern coast of France. The weather changed rapidly, and he found the rough water challenging.

Monet worked quickly in order to capture a moment. *Storm off the Belle-Isle Coast* is a darker painting from this time. Yet, it shows Monet's admiration for beauty and colors.

Storm off the Belle-Isle Coast *is one of Monet's many Belle-Isle seascapes. Several of these were included together in a Paris exhibition in spring 1887.*

Water Garden

In addition to challenging the boundaries of art, Monet also experimented with new ways to display his work. In 1891, he exhibited a group of paintings with a common theme. He enjoyed great success with his grain stacks series. Each individual painting was beautiful. But being surrounded by all of the paintings created a completely new experience for the audience.

Around the time of Monet's show, Ernest Hoschedé died. On July 16, 1892, Monet married Alice Hoschedé. The following year, Monet began construction on a water garden at his home in Giverny. The garden had a bridge and a large pond filled with water lilies. It was inspired by Japanese gardens. After Monet's garden was completed, people worldwide came to admire its beauty.

In January 1895, Monet traveled to Norway. He found the local mountains very beautiful. Monet painted several views of Mount Kolsaas. These works were influenced by Japanese prints.

Artist's Corner

Monet was one of the leaders of the Impressionist movement. The Impressionists wanted to capture scenes as they happened. To do this, they often painted outdoors. They also tried to show the way light changed an object's appearance.

These Impressionist themes can be seen in Monet's series paintings. Over the years, Monet painted series on the Saint-Lazare train station, Rouen Cathedral, the Houses of Parliament in London, and a row of poplar trees. In the early 1890s, Monet painted his grain stacks series *(below)* in Giverny. In each painting, the subject remains the same. The main difference between the works is the lighting.

Like other Impressionists, Monet had been loyal to the plein air painting method. He often completed entire paintings outdoors. But for his series paintings, Monet began finishing works in his studio. In this way, he could look at all the paintings at once. Then, he could slightly alter the works to make each painting link to the next.

Traveling

Monet continued traveling. Over the years, he visited England, Italy, and Switzerland. Everywhere he went, he painted. Monet was amazed at the variety he found in the world.

After each trip, Monet returned to Giverny. There, he found happiness painting in his gardens. Between 1900 and 1926, Monet created more than 250 garden-themed paintings. He continued to be fascinated by reflections in water.

Many of Monet's garden paintings were of water lilies. He prepared a series of water lily paintings for an exhibition at the Durand-Ruel Gallery. Monet made sure that the paintings would be shown as a group. A successful exhibition of 48 water lily works finally opened in May 1909.

But soon, tragedy struck Monet. Alice died in 1911. Monet's son Jean died three years later. After their deaths, Monet traveled less. Instead, younger artists such as Pierre Bonnard, Édouard Vuillard, and Henri Matisse visited him at his home.

Monet exhibited four
circular water lily paintings
at the Durand-Ruel Gallery.

Claude Monet 1907

New Appreciation

After **World War I** began in 1914, Monet continued to work from his gardens. The fighting was close enough to hear, but Monet stayed in Giverny. There, he created a large-scale set of water lily paintings.

The French government accepted the water lilies project in 1922. A special room was set aside at the Orangerie, now the Musée de l'Orangerie, in Paris. The 22 paintings celebrated the end of World War I. But just like after the **Franco-Prussian War**, people wanted change. Monet's popularity was falling.

To add to his problems, Monet had **cataracts**. He was going blind, but he kept painting. Even after an operation in 1923, his vision never fully returned. He especially had trouble with colors. Monet's last paintings were modern-looking swirls of colors and brushstrokes.

Monet died in Giverny on December 5, 1926. His career ended as it had begun, with few admirers. But years later, people started to realize how much Monet had contributed to the art world. Today, Monet is an inspiration to many artists.

Monet in his studio with the water lily paintings

Glossary

caricature - a type of cartoonish drawing that makes certain parts of the subject appear bigger and others smaller.

cataract - a clouding of the lens of the eye. This condition obstructs the passage of light through the eye and can result in blindness.

commission - a request to complete a work, such as a painting, for a certain person. To be commissioned is to be given such a request.

critic - a professional who gives his or her opinion on art or performances.

draft - to select for military service. People who are drafted must serve in the armed forces.

Franco-Prussian War - from 1870 to 1871. A war fought between France and Prussia, a former kingdom now in Germany. Prussia won the war and created the German Empire.

genre - a category of art, music, or literature.

plein air - painting outdoors, especially relating to a branch of Impressionism that focuses on representing outdoor light and air.

rebel - a person who disobeys authority or the government.

World War I - from 1914 to 1918, fought in Europe. Great Britain, France, Russia, the United States, and their allies were on one side. Germany, Austria-Hungary, and their allies were on the other side.

Saying It

Alfred Sisley - awl-frehd see-slay
Camille Pissarro - kaw-meey pee-saw-roh
Charles-François Daubigny - shawrl-frahn-swaw doh-been-yee
Eugène-Louis Boudin - oo-zhan-lwee boo-dan
Le Havre - luh HAHVRUH
Pierre-Auguste Renoir - pyehr-aw-goost ruhn-wawr
Seine - SEHN
Thames - TEHMZ

Web Sites

To learn more about Claude Monet, visit ABDO Publishing Company on the World Wide Web at **www.abdopublishing.com**. Web sites about Monet are featured on our Book Links page. These links are routinely monitored and updated to provide the most current information available.

Index